Longs Peak, Rocky Mountain National Park
Painting by Albert Bierstadt
Courtesy The Denver Public Library, Western History Collection

"This is not my native country but everything in it tells me who I am."

– Wallace Stegner

Destination Colorado

Colorado sits in the western half of the United States at the east-central edge of the Rocky Mountain region and at the western edge of the Great Plains. In Spanish Colorado means "colored red." Colorado's climate is mild and semiarid and offers 296 days of sunshine per year. The Capitol City is Denver. About 4,175,003 people now live in the state, which means that the population has almost quadrupled since 1940. Congress established the Territory of Colorado in 1861, and its constitution was written in 1876. The center of the state is approximately 1,850 miles west of the Eastern Coast, 1,250 miles from the West Coast, 675 miles from Mexico and 850 miles from Canada. Colorado's closest neighbors are Kansas and Nebraska to the east, Nebraska and Wyoming to the north, Utah to the west, and New Mexico and Oklahoma to the south. The boundary lines create an almost perfect rectangle that measures approximately 387 miles from east to west and 276 miles from north to south. It covers 104,247 square miles, and 450 of those miles are bodies of water. Colorado is the eighth largest state in square miles. Colorado is the tallest state, with an average elevation of 6,800 feet above sea level. The lowest point, 3,350 feet above sea level, is near the town of Holly at the Arkansas River, and the highest point is the summit of Mt. Elbert which measures 14,431 feet, or 2.72 miles, above sea level. Colorado is home to 54 peaks over 14,000 feet high, 55 national parks, forests and monuments, and the headwaters to six major rivers. Over a third of the state's land (66.7 million acres) is forest. The state animal is the Big Horn Sheep; the state bird is the Lark Bunting; the state fish is the Greenback Cut Throat Trout. Colorado's state flower is the white or lavender Columbine; the state tree is the Colorado Blue Spruce; the state fossil is the Stegosaurus and the state gemstone is the Aquamarine.

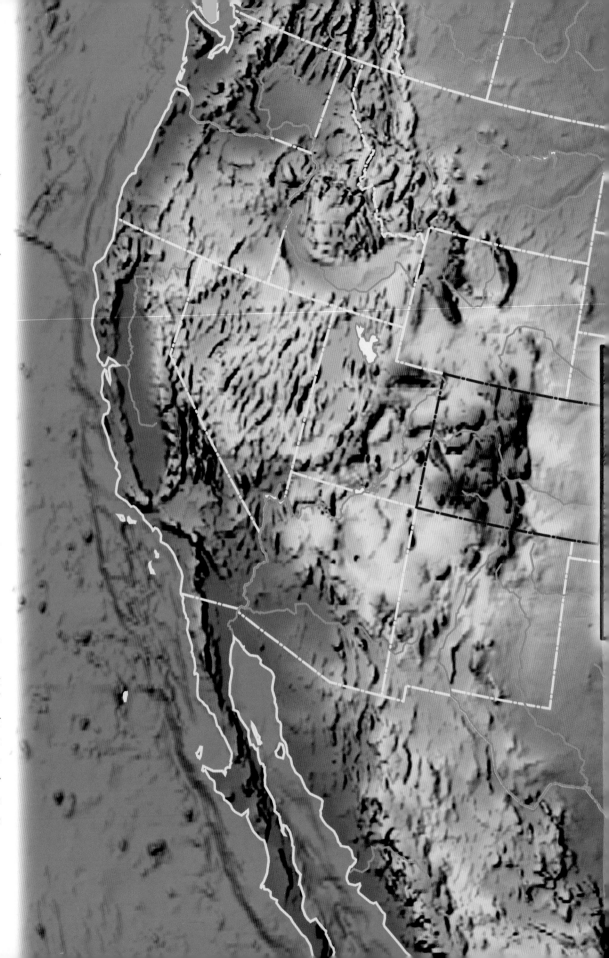

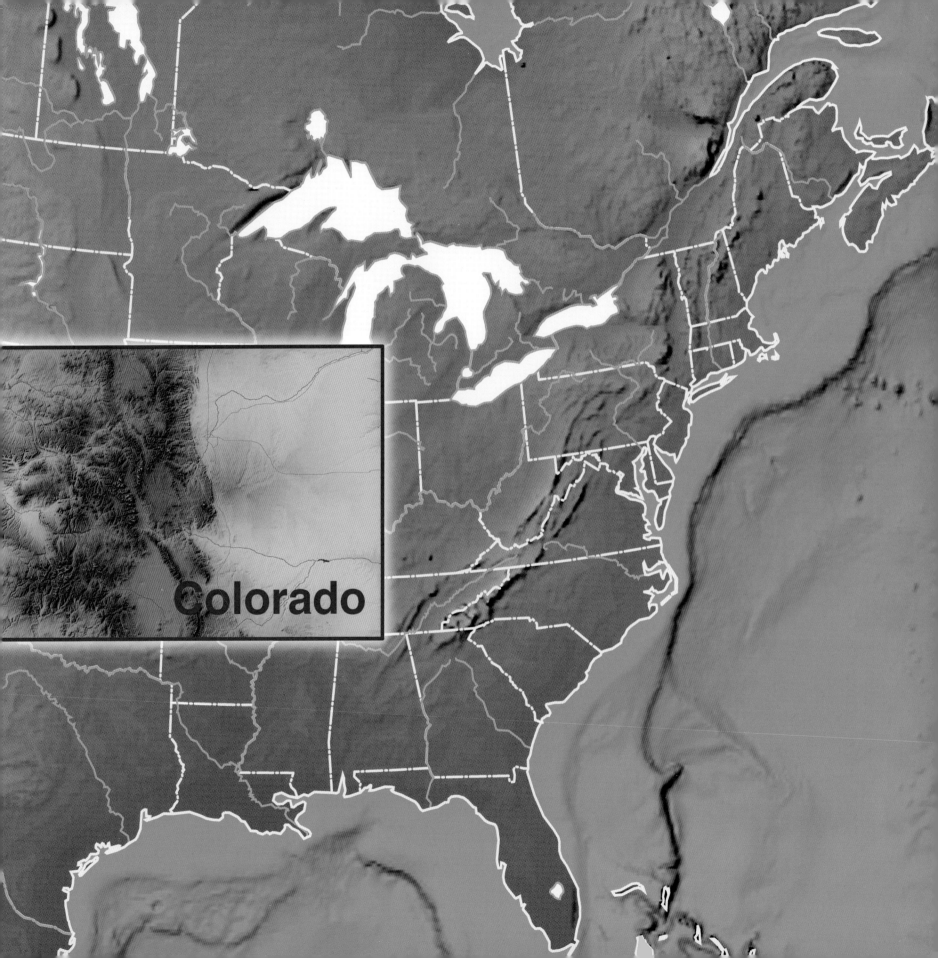

Colorado

Spring Snow–Maroon Bells

COLORADO
Heart & Soul

Story & Photography by
Robert Castellino

Introduction by
Mark Udall

Silver Jack Reservoir–Umcompahgre National Forest

Whispering River, LLC
Boulder, Colorado
Phone (303) 440-7711
Fax (303) 440-3431

Robert Castellino, *Publisher*

Designed by Dave Dombrowski, Elizabeth O. Taylor, Susan Szvada, & Len Krueger
Edited by Geri Lynn Baumblatt

Printed and Bound in China
through Palace Press International
ISBN 1-879914-53-0 (Paperback)
ISBN 1-879914-52-2 (Hardcover)

Library of Congress Card Catalog Number: 99-093646

First Printing, 1999

Dedication

This book is dedicated to all those who have shaped the heart and soul of Colorado through their vision, desire and devotion to maintain its historical character, natural beauty and way of life in the West to make Colorado our home.

For my Son, Joren

Deer Lodge Park–Dinosaur National Monument

TABLE OF CONTENTS

INTRODUCTION

Mark Udall
United States Representative
Colorado, 1999

As a native Westerner, I have a deep personal and spiritual connection to Colorado. While a young man, my grandfather was a cowboy and later was the first outfitter (with a horsepacking business) in Rocky Mountain National Park. As an adult, I have explored, with what might be thought of as religious fervor, Colorado's high mountains, rivers, prairies and canyons. Many years I've spent more nights sleeping under the stars than under a roof. Together with my wife, Maggie, we have hiked, skied and kayaked across our great state. Now, as a parent, because of Colorado's natural bounty, I could not think of a better place to raise my children.

In these pages, Robert Castellino captures the wonder and spirit of Colorado and gives you a sense of the unparalleled beauty of our natural landscape. You can visualize the diversity of our ecosystems, from the majestic mountains to the wild rivers and vibrant red canyons. You can feel the change of the seasons, from the clear, crisp winter nights to the warm, dry summers. And you can begin to understand the vast openness that gives us all a sense of endless possibility.

Today, we in Colorado find ourselves at a crossroads. Predictions forecast that the population of Colorado will double in the next forty years. How we proceed with regard to finding a balance between economic development and prosperity and preserving our natural environment will affect not only where we live, but who we are.

What makes Colorado so special is also what presents us with our greatest challenge. The very place we are drawn to for its clean air, great skies, and natural beauty is now in danger. The landscape that we treasure is changing, and our unique challenge is to manage our growth while maintaining our economy and accommodating the people who want to live here for the quality of life Colorado provides.

The beautiful images and stories in this book remind us that every day we must rededicate ourselves to preserving Colorado's heart and soul. I am mindful of the old adage: "We do not inherit the earth from our parents, but rather we borrow it from our children." We owe it to our children, grandchildren, and future generations to preserve our natural landscape, to teach them the countless lessons contained in our surroundings, and to instill in them a sense of responsibility and stewardship for this magical place.

Gazing into the Sunrise at Red Rocks Park–Morrison

"*We sang songs that carried in their melodies all the sounds of nature —
the running of waters, the sighing of winds, and the calls of the animals.
Teach these to your children that they may come to love nature as we love it.*"

— Grand Council Fire of American Indians to the Mayor of Chicago
December 1927

Needles Mountains from Animas Canyon
Photographer: W.H. Jackson
Courtesy of The Denver Public Library, Western History Collection

Colorado History

Colorado's Celebrated Native American Heritage

DID THEY TRAVERSE THE NORTHERN PACIFIC by boat or walk on barren strips of ice from Siberia? Did they migrate north from South America, or have Native Americans always lived here? Maybe they were born out of the creation of the underworld as their ancestors say. These questions are the roots of theories that lead us to postulate how Native Americans came to be in Colorado and North America. Archaelogical sites, radiocarbon traces and prehistoric artifacts led scientists to form a picture of life as it was over many thousands of years.

Roughly twelve thousand years ago, Paleo-Indians lived in this region in a much cooler climate where high, alpine glaciers extended through mountain valleys down towards the plains. According to Sally Crum, author of *People of the Red Earth: American Indians of Colorado*, "Streams flowed into the plains where grasslands with lakes supported giant sloths and beavers, large herds of mammoths, mastodons, giant bison, camels, horses, elk, deer, antelope, bighorn sheep and other species."

These people were hunter-gatherers. The Clovis and Folsom people are considered the first culture to inhabit the New World in Colorado. Sometime around ten thousand B.P. ("before the present"), the Plano people evolved as the climate changed and larger species became extinct. Archaeological findings indicate longer and narrower arrowheads attached to spear shafts with throwing Atlatl were invented by the Plano for hunting large game, which was the main source of protein in their diet. According to Crum, "women not only butchered and prepared the meat, hides and clothing, but spent much of their time gathering wild fruits, roots, nuts and seeds. They dried fruit, cooked the roots, and shelled nuts; the seeds were used to make mush, breads and cakes."

Around seven thousand B.P., Archaic people roamed this land, followed herds and lived in pit houses. They snared small game, hunted larger game, foraged and became farmers. Traces of their evolution are found in pit dwellings above the Colorado River at Battlement Mesa, at Yarmony, north near Rangely and Maybell, and down along the Gunnison River where the Blue Mesa Reservoir now fills the valley. The climate for the next three to five thousand years was drier and forced the Archaic people to higher mountainous altitudes in search of food and water. Most notably, the pit houses were somewhat inhabitable, semi-permanent dwellings where the origins of the Basketmaker people lie. They wove baskets from Indian Hemp, Yucca and clay. Basketmakers were the predecessors to the infamous Pueblo Anasazi who are known for their cliff dwellings in Mesa Verde.

"Pueblo" means "village" and "Anasazi" means "ancient ones." Most importantly, sandals woven from Indian Hemp and Yucca made walking much easier, and have been found throughout the southwest corner of the state. The Fremont people of the northern great basin out along the Yampa and Green Rivers are thought to have splintered off from the Anasazi. It is thought that the Anasazi disappeared with the drought in the mid 1200's A.D. They are best known for their sophisticated apartment-like complexes built on mesa tops and under the overhangs of the slick-rock canyon walls. Far from the mountains and out to the East, the prehistoric plains and woodland people known as the Upper Republican and Apishapa cultures, were making their mark as nomadic hunters, gatherers and farmers. Their lives were centered around the migratory routes of game and the changing seasons. They used wickiups to move their belongings and themselves across vast sections of grassland. They too followed a similar evolutionary path as that of the Freemonts and Anasazi. As time passed, these people disappeared with the last years of the 1200's

Ute mother with her baby secured to a cradleboard—Garden of the Gods, 1911
Photograph Courtesy of The Denver Public Library, Western History Collection

as the drought drove them south to their cultural center near the Four Corners and Chaco Canyon in New Mexico.

The myths and lore of the ancient Freemont people, Anasazi, Arapaho, Cheyenne, Kiowa Ute, Apache, Sioux, and Pawnee echo through the walls of slick-rock canyons, out to high country meadows and across the prairie grasslands of Colorado. Their legacy is a powerful part of our lives today. What little is known of their past, paints a picture of people who lived in harmony with nature and honored the spirit of their ancestry. Compared to the lives of modern city dwellers, life was a struggle for survival. Average life expectancy was 35 to 50 years. These semi-nomadic tribes and cliff-dwellers moved where they needed to as the seasons changed. They lived according to their tribes' ceremonial rituals. They understood their place in the cosmos, revered their elders and tended to their youths' growth with a deep reverence for the inheritance they left to future generations. They were artisans, spirit keepers, truth sayers, storytellers, shamans, magicians, cooks, tricksters, painters, dancers, sculptors, stonemasons, basket makers, potters, weavers, seamstresses, architects, irrigators, traders, river guides, trackers, messengers, horse trainers, peacemakers and warriors. These people were steeped in traditions and believed the earth did not belong to them. They felt a part of a great mystery which granted them life on earth. This primary understanding of their own existence is a common thread that runs through all of these cultures and sets them apart from the Anglo-European explorers, settlers and gold seekers they would soon encounter.

Ute women construct a tepee at Garden of the Gods, El Paso County, Colorado.
Photograph Courtesy of The Denver Public Library, Western History Collection

"Grand Father, I thank the Great Spirit, the Sun and the Moon, for putting me on this earth. It is a good earth, and I hope there will be no more fighting on it—that the grass will grow and the water fall, and plenty of buffalo. You, Grand Father, are doing well for your children, in coming so far and taking so much trouble about them.

I think you will do us much good; I will go home satisfied. I will sleep sound, and not have to watch my horses in the night, nor be afraid for my (family). We have to live on these streams and in the hills, and I would be glad if the whites would pick out a place for themselves and not come into our grounds; but if they must pass through our country, they should give us game for what they drive off."

– Chief Cut Nose, Arapaho addressing the tribal nations at the 1851 Council with US Government at Fort Laramie

Ute mother, Amy Kent and her daughter walk across a grassy field at Monument Valley Park, El Paso County, Colorado. (August, 1912) Photograph Courtesy of The Denver Public Library, Western History Collection

Circa 1913. Photograph Courtesy of The Denver Public Library, Western History Collection

Native American Utes, including Edwin Cloud and George Norris, are in a line on horseback en route to the reburial of the remains of Chief Ouray, near Ignacio, Colorado.

Changing of Hands–Colorado's Transition Years

MIDWAY THROUGH THE NINETEENTH CENTURY, the wide open landscape that the indigenous natives had known as their ground forever changed as Anglo-Europeans flooded into Colorado to seek the spoils of gold and silver. It was not just the rush for riches that brought on the fighting, but a clear contrast in values that separated their ways of life. The Anglo-Europeans brought with them their belief in Manifest Destiny, that this was their "eminent domain" to have as they chose by the making of their own laws. In contrast, the native peoples lived by the humble laws of nature. Ownership of land was at stake as mining claims and settlers established their homesteads. Although it was common knowledge that a few of the native cultures had territorial skirmishes with each other, greater pressures came from the U.S. Army who wanted to settle the territory on behalf of the government; this became the center of the Ute's, Cheyenne's, and Arapahoe's disastrous decimation. Broken treaty after broken treaty, the U.S. government angered the native people as they rooted them from their land and moved them to less inhabitable locales.

On the cold morning of November 29, 1864, Colonel John M. Chivington, along with civilian volunteers from Denver, rode into the peaceful, sleeping village of Cheyenne and Arapahoe at Sand Creek. The massacre that morning sent a chilling message to all tribes. Such a savage retaliation to rid this land of Indians was one of the harshest moments in the history of the West. 137 native people perished that morning. Among the dead were 109 women and children.

Throughout Colorado, martial law prevailed for the next two years. Ultimately, the Cheyenne and Arapahoe signed the Medicine Lodge Treaty that made them dependent on the government and banished them to Oklahoma. According to Sally Crum in *People of the Red Earth, Life in Indian Territory*, "life was not pleasant for the tribes that had formerly ranged along the mountains and rivers of eastern Colorado. Starving people in Indian Territory were often forced to kill their horses to survive. All tribal populations declined drastically." Depending on who spoke, whether it was an Anglo settler or an elderly tribeswoman, the stories varied greatly in content and tone. There is no doubt that the best of life as the natives had known it had forever disappeared to benefit the newcomers who were here to tame the wild.

Colorado's Anglo-European Heritage

IN 1541, SPANISH EXPLORER DON FRANCISCO Vasquez de Coronado, on a campaign to find gold for his homeland, crossed through southern Colorado on his return to Mexico from a two-year campaign through the southwest. Later, in 1779, Don Juan Bautista de Anza and his 573 men pushed north out of Sante Fe through the San Luis Valley across South Park and over the foothills of the front range to the eastern plains. They fought battles with Comanches and Utes to establish their position. By 1878, the Spaniards had established a small settlement named San Carlos in the Arkansas Valley near the present day city of Pueblo. According to Ubbelohde, Benson and Smith, authors of *A Colorado History*, "From Coronado in 1540 to short-lived San Carlos in 1787, Spain failed to push its settlements north of Sante Fe."

In 1803, the United States doubled its size with a bargain of acquisitions from the Spaniards in the Louisiana Territory. A young aspiring Lieutenant, Zebulon Montgomery Pike, led a small expedition of twenty-two men into Colorado, "to observe the geography, natural history, and topography, and to collect mineral and botanical specimens," as related by Ubbelohde, Benson and Smith. Pike's efforts did not match his plan to find the headwaters of the Arkansas and Red rivers. Yet his journal-logged accounts were a valuable source of information about the geography and natural resources in Colorado. His report was published in 1810 and received wide acclaim in the United States and Europe. His hope to climb Pikes Peak (named after him) failed when waist-deep snow thwarted his effort. Following in Pike's footsteps was Major Stephen H. Long who was commissioned to search out the source of the Arkansas and explore the high climbs of the Rockies. Although he was comissioned to survey a general area, Long failed to

find the origin of the Arkansas or map the Red River. His report that the plains east of the Rocky Mountains were a sandy, arid desert lived on far past his death and discouraged generations of easterners from marching West.

Ultimately, the next fifty years were years of transition. Trappers came to exploit the rivers' beaver populations. Others explored the uncharted territory and led the way for pioneers to find their way west on the Oregon and Sante Fe Trails. The U.S. government sponsored troops that marched to protect the expansion of the West for the first miners and settlers. The momentum of the westward movement could be read on pioneers' wagons: "Pikes Peak or bust."

By the mid to late 1850's, the first wave of westward-seeking pioneers came to Colorado in search of gold. The lore of mining towns springing up overnight was sung from every gulch where a claim was laid. Not only were there struggles with the "hostile Indians," there were differences between miners about claims and land ownership. The lawless mining camps became more civilized, and out in the plains in towns like Denver, Manifest Destiny finally caught up with Colorado as more and more people came to lay their claims and settle. The Colorado Territory was established in 1861 with the same boundaries which define the state today. With the native people removed from the plains and out of the mountain heights by the late 1860's, the settlement of Colorado was growing out of its infancy. Civilization was upon Colorado in a heartbeat. Railroads connected the major east, west, north and south routes into Denver. Colorado College in Colorado Springs, and the University of Colorado at Boulder were founded. Lead carbonate ores, rich in silver, were found near Leadville. Leadville

Wheat field (probably in Roaring Fork River valley near Carbondale, Colorado), reached via Colorado Midland Railway; shows two men standing in waist-deep field inspecting heads of wheat. (between 1900 and 1910) Photograph Courtesy of The Denver Public Library, Western History Collection.

View of a Colorado Central narrow gauge train on Devil's Gate High Bridge (300 feet long, 96 feet above Clear Creek, set on a two percent grade) Clear Creek County, Colorado. The Loop winds its way between Georgetown and Silver Plume. (Between 1884 and 1895), Photograph Courtesy of The Denver Public Library, Western History Collection

bragged the finest red-light district in the United States. Grand stories of mining towns rang from the mountains, and anybody who could found their way to stake a claim. Not all were to find their way to riches though. Colorado became the 38th State admitted to the Union in 1876 and the cycles of boom and bust began to develop a pattern that would follow Colorado's future into the twentieth century. By 1900 the state's population reached 539,700. By 1910 there were 49,170 farms dotting the eastern plains and western slope. The state's population had jumped to 799,024 in a ten-year period, and by the year 1920 Colorado had grown to 939,629. Fortunately, vast tracts of wild lands were set aside as parks and monuments. The wide open wild west was well established as a part of Colorado's landscape. These were self-reliant people; the men were rugged individualists, and the women were strong and resourceful. Oftentimes, they moved behind the scenes to make way for Colorado's growth. The openness of the West shaped their lives and futures.

Today, on the eve of the twenty-first century, Colorado is one of the fastest growing regions in the United States. Every modern technological convenience and opportunity await those who make Colorado their home. Our heritage is rooted in the people who mined, homesteaded, farmed, developed and protected this land and all of its natural beauty. Cities and towns throughout Colorado are fed by a steady stream of visitors who come here to enjoy the pleasures of a wide range of outdoor activities. We are proud of this place and of the home we have made; it is built on a rich legacy from the archives of the romantic history of the West.

View of the Crystal Mill powerhouse built in 1893, on Crystal River; shows the wooden dam with a raised water level and the wooden shaft that turns the waterwheel; rooftops of the wood frame structures of Crystal City, Colorado in the distance. (1893) Photograph Courtesy of The Denver Public Library, Western History Collection

Swimmers frolic in the Natatorium of the Hot Springs Lodge and Pool at Glenwood Springs, Colorado in Garfield County. (Between 1925 and 1930) Photograph Courtesy of The Denver Public Library, Western History Collection

Welcome Arch, Union Station, Denver, Colorado. The Welcome Arch was torn down in 1931when it was deemed a traffic hazard. (Between 1906 and 1910)
Photograph Courtesy of The Denver Public Library, Western History Collection

View of Colorado State Capitol and grounds. Capitol dome with gold-leaf completed in 1908 Denver, Colorado (Between 1908 and 1910),
Photograph Courtesy of The Denver Public Library, Western History Collection

Colorado's Changing Seasons

WHEREVER YOU FIND YOURSELF IN COLORADO, the seasonal changes are indelibly etched into our daily lives as they are marked on the calendar throughout the year. Beyond the shifting weather patterns that define each season are the subtle effects in nature that illustrate all of its magnificence. These changes are as unique in character to the seasons they portray as they are to the diverse bioregions known around the state. From the prairie grasslands on the high eastern plains to the heights of the Rockies along the Continental Divide and out to the desert that stretches from north to southwest, the changing seasons are separated more definitively by the landscape than by the celebrated annual equinoxes. As the temperature fluctuates and weather changes, we concern ourselves more with the attire we wear and often forget the effect the changing seasons have on us. Beyond our daily and worldly concerns, out in nature we begin to experience and understand these subtle seasons of change.

Early on, winter covers the land with cold, white snow. Later, as its length wears on, dark shadows of brown and gray appear. The coral glow of a winter sunrise illuminates the heights of the Divide, then disappears as swiftly as it made its claim to the new day's dawn. A frigid, arctic wind rolls through the canyons and valleys and scours the grasslands on the plains. We draw into our homes; we huddle close with our families and tighten the bonds with our dearest friends. We tend to our hearth's low burning fire. We draw deeper into our soul's journey as the longest night casts its dark mid-winter spell. Are we any different from nature's own, who seek safekeeping from winter's wrath inside their dens? The hard, cold edge held through these shortened days gives way to mid-winter thaws. For a moment, we waken to the possibilities waiting just ahead. The final surges of winter draw us

Indian Paint Brush—The Yampa River

Heart Lake Drainage—Indian Peaks Wilderness

The Changing Seasons

Aspen Stand–McClure Pass

Maroon Bells Wilderness from Loge Peak

in a few last times. The earth is marked white and saturated with the dew of tomorrow's hope. Finally, the snows fade into our long winter dreams. The season changes.

The lush, wet rains of spring run together with the flooding, snowmelt currents of rivers and streams from high above. All around our cities and towns the new warmth of spring emerges. Flourishes of greens, yellows, and reds pour forth. Everything appears to blossom at once. Our eyes are widened by the burst of colors. Nature oozes around us and our nostrils fill with smells of sweet nectar. Our own internal workings are jilted as we feel our juices flowing strong. Startled from the dance with spring's intimate offering, a Chinook blows hard, raising our brow against the old feelings of winter's angst. We push back in return, longing for the richness broken by this gusty burst. In the wind's wake,

the fresh air helps us sigh a welcome breath of relief from spring's languid hold on our presence. We remember that something is happening outside of our bodily senses. Not far away, nature stirs in the wild to her own rhythm. Sounds of Meadow Lark at dawn call us to this new day. The buzz of hummingbirds and bees fill the air as they dart from blossom to blossom. Do we move to the same pattern as that of the wildlife now emerging into the open? A great sense of awe sets into the tone of our awareness. We settle

into long, warm days that draw us out into the high, thin air of Colorado activities. The season changes again.

The pulse of summer's intensity bears the baking heat of midday sun. Morning and afternoon thundershowers break from the skies and we bask in their cool reprieve. Children scurry off to camp, soccer practice and music lessons; they return from their activities to reap the blessings of warm evenings at play in the neighborhood. A bursting sunset blazes across the evening sky above Colorado's Rocky Mountains. Have you ever seen it rain fire in the sky? To escape the heat's intensity, many exit the cities en masse for cooler climbs in mountain country. Once, not too long ago, we sat by a stream or lake, attended a Chautauqua concert, hiked into a lush mountain meadow, or sang by a campfire taking in the expanse of the Milky Way. Many have pondered what lies beyond those stars, beyond this world we inhabit. At such inspired moments, those with grand imaginations and their own visions rose to chase their dreams. At other times, the night sounds of nature's creatures scurrying by or calling out into the depths of the darkness sends a chill up your spine. The higher we climb into the mountains, the more summer appears as spring in the lower altitudes. The dogged heat and our work-a-day world beg us to pursue the last warm summer's evening to rest and rejuvenate. Moved or pulled by summer's call, we give ourselves over to its pleasures until the days begin to shorten. The foliage burned, the dry earth thirsts for one last summer rain. Nature's own begin to store their annual forage. We make one last pilgrimage to escape the urban bustle, and summer turns to fall.

Coolness fills the autumn calm, almost as if Nature herself staged one last curtain call. Stillness resides in the halls of Colorado's landscape. Sunrise brings first frosts glistening across withering ground cover as the memory of hot summer afternoons fades in the shortened evening hours. Nature retreats on command, drawing in and turning away from the activity of life. For a while, the colors turn to glowing golds, ambers and reds. Against an azure evening sky, the alpen glow of golden Aspen leaves illuminates every crevasse along canyon walls. The air weighs heavy; the rivers run slow, clear and low. The Canada Geese, Sandhill Cranes and Mallard Ducks migrate south through the San Luis Valley. A great harvest moon rises into the evening sky over the eastern plains. The wind blows strong, a signal that winter knocks at our door, as cold creeps in from reaches further north. The colors fall to the earth and, as the first snow blankets Colorado, we realize the changes of another year.

Waterlily–Surprise Lake, The Gore Range

"Nobody sees a flower—
really—
it is so small it takes time—
we haven't time—
and to see takes time,
like to have a friend takes time."

—GEORGIA O'KEEFFE

Shooting Stars–Mt. Zerkel Wilderness

Wild Poppy–McClintock Trail, Boulder Mountain Parks

Wild Flower–Lake Isabelle Drainage, Indian Peaks Wilderness

Colorado Columbine

Wild Lily–Eldorado Springs State Park

"*Most new discoveries are suddenly–seen things*
that were always there."

– SUSAN K. LANGER

Wild Poppy–McClintock Trail, Boulder Mountain Parks

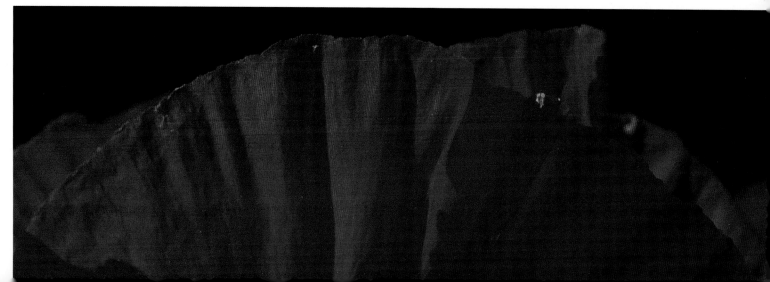

"A cloud does not know why it moves in just such a direction and at such a speed. It feels impulsion . . . this is the place to go now. But the sky knows the reasons and the patterns behind all clouds and you will know, too, when you high enough to see beyond horizons."

– Richard Bach

t yourself

Westerly View from LaPlata Peak–Collegiate Peaks Wilderness

Water Berries–Cataract Falls, The Gore Range

"There is more here than meets the eye."

–LADY MURASAKI

Fire Weed–The Cimmaron River Drainage

Wheeler Lakes—The Gore Range

Poison Ivy–Boulder Mountain Parks

Floating Leaves–Boulder Mountain Parks

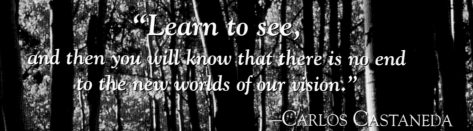

"Learn to see,
and then you will know that there is no end
to the new worlds of our vision."

—CARLOS CASTANEDA

Reflection on Maroon Lake–Maroon Bells Wilderness

Cottonwood & Leaf–Boulder Mountain Parks

Sievers Mountain, Maroon Bells–Snowmass Wilderness

Cimmaron River Valley–Big Blue Wilderness

Fall on the Elk River near Steamboat Springs

Bear Canyon–Boulder Mountain Parks

"*In Wildness is the preservation of the World.*"
–Henry David Thoreau

Autumn Reflection–Maroon Lake, Maroon Bells Wilderness

"What a lovely surprise to discover how un-lonely being alone can be."

—ELLEN BURSTYN

Lone Pine in Snow–Red Mountain Pass

Mount Sopris, Maroon Bells–Snowmass Wilderness

Mount Sneffels from Telluride

Jacque Peak & Ridge–The Gore Range

41

Supple Winterscape near Silverton

Snow laden Cottonwoods along Boulder Creek

Shadow Aspen–The Grand Mesa

Water & Ice–Maroon Creek

"Change is inevitable.
It shapes those who accept it
and it breaks those who don't.

The seasons of change are all around changing what we
cannot see in ourselves that appears so obvious to others."

–ROBERT L. CASTELLINO

14,000 Foot Little Bear Peak, Ellingwood Point, Blanca Peak and Mount Lindsey–Sangre De Cristo Mountains

Sunset Across Mount of the Holy Cross Wilderness from China Bowl at Vail Resort

C.W. Buccholz, Executive Director
Rocky Mountain National Park Association
Sunrise at Moraine Park

*"The pursuit of truth and beauty is a sphere of activity in
which we are permitted to remain children all our lives."*

—ALBERT EINSTEIN

Colorado Heart & Soul

Colorado's Heart & Soul

FEW COLORADANS YOU EVER MEET ARE NATIVE, but everyone, no matter how long they have lived here, will tell you how much they love Colorado. People are drawn to the mountains and to the outdoor life of "the High Country." There is something special about Colorado and its people. Maybe it's the easy pace of the westerner, the thin air that slows things down, or the warm, friendly smile when a passerby says, "hello." Perhaps it's the immense, blue-sky days that give you the sense of the great expanse, or maybe it's the everpresent sense of adventure. Out on the eastern plains lives the old-time farmer who tells stories of how Colorado used to be and gives you a sense of what you missed out on back in the good old days. Here, as in many places in the West, the myths and legends of yesterday linger in the character and architecture of our towns.

Whether this is your first visit, or whether you have lived here for a lifetime, no one can deny that Colorado kindles the imagination. It is a thirst that cannot be quenched, it is the love of this place and of the great outdoors. There is no mistaking the passion for life of those who make their home in the heart and soul of Colorado.

People are the heart of Colorado. Their character can be as rugged as the jagged edge along the high divide. Turn another corner, and the people are as embracing as the breathtaking beauty waiting just around the bend; they are open and genuine. A voice resonates in the mountain air and welcomes visitors from all walks of life.

You might find us at the rodeo on a summer's night in Steamboat, perusing the art at the festival in Cherry Creek, running the Bolder Boulder, skiing the West Wall at A-Basin, tying flies in the Cowdry Cafe, hobnobbing at the Aspen Music Festival, climbing the 14,000-foot Crestone Needle, rafting Browns Canyon on the Arkansas, sailing on Dillon Resevoir, back-country skiing to the Polar Star Hut, coaching a junior soccer game, camping along the Poudre, taking in an play at the Denver Performing Arts Center,

contemplating the Anasazi cliff dwellings in Mesa Verde, listening in on a ranger's talk at Rocky Mountain National Park, pondering the digs at Dinosaur National Monument, mountain-biking in the Rockies, rooting on the Broncos at Mile High Stadium, backpacking in the Flat Tops, strolling down Main Street in Telluride, hiking the Colorado Trail, horseback riding across the Sand Dunes National Monument, taking in a concert at Red Rocks Amphitheater, kicking back in Pagosa Hot Springs or riding the narrow gauge from Durango to Silverton. In every part of its grand expanse, Coloradans live for the outdoors.

Then there are stories of hardrock miners, unsung women, farmers and ranchers who passed through and settled in Colorado when it was still the wild west. These people are a part of the legacy that remain at the core of Colorado. Today there is a community of people in the towns and cities across this state that graciously serve as volunteers and leaders. They work to preserve the wildlife and open spaces, and their work often goes unrewarded. There is no accounting for their efforts or generosity, and there is never enough praise or thanks for their devotion. They make the difference, and they make Colorado our home.

The expansive landscape where we live and play is the soul of Colorado. The diverse beauty gives rise to the character that makes Colorado unique. There are slick, rock desert canyons, endless prairie grasslands, wild, free-flowing rivers, massive peaks, great pine forests, high plateaus, intimate meadows, groves of ageless Aspen, geothermic hot springs, wind-worn arches, clear-water lakes and night skies filled with stars. From the heart of our cities and neighborhood streets, the backcountry roads lead us to these phenomenal open spaces. These places are the link to our natural heritage. Not only do we play and live in them, we protect them with a fervency that inspires the most sensitive souls to join forces in assuring their preservation. Without these precious wild places, we would soon find Coloradans grasping for the core values that are the soul of our existence now and for generations to come.

Summer Afternoon–Cataract Lake

Painting Poppies–Chautaqua Park

"*I go to nature to be soothed and healed, and to have my senses put in order.*"
–JOHN BURROUGHS

Sprouting Rock–Hanging Lake in Glennwood Canyon

Sunrise at Deer Lodge Park–Yampa River

Cowboys in the Chutes at
Steamboat Springs

Walking the Line–Yampa, Colorado

"Her name won't be in history books,
This women of the land;
Her heart is where it wants to be,
Content with Heaven's plan."
–GWEN PETERSON

Bucking Bronco–Steamboat Rodeo

53

Kayaking Number 6–The Arkansas River

Kayaker–The Numbers, The Arkansas River

*"There are no passengers on spaceship earth.
We are all crew."*

–MARSHALL MCLUHAN

The Royal Gorge–Arkansas River

> *"Let the beauty we love be what we do."*
>
> –Rumi

Scouting Warm Springs Rapid–the Yampa

Arch I–Rattlesnake Canyon

River Sage—The Yampa River

One with the Rock—Estes Park

Deer Lodge Park–The Yampa

Amazed–The Great Tiger Wall

"*Security is mostly a superstition.*
It does not exist in nature, nor do the children of men as a whole experience it.
Avoiding danger is no safer in the long run than outright exposure.
Life is either a daring adventure or nothing."

–HELEN KELLER

Climber at the Diamond–Longs Peak

Hikers at Dinosaur National Monument

Repelling off the Maiden

"I will tell you what I have learned myself.
For me, a long five or six mile walk helps.
And one must go alone and everyday."

–BRENDA UELAND

60

Sailing Dillon Reservoir–Summit County

Sailing Frisco Bay–Dillon Reservoir

Tenth Mountain Hut

64

Skier at Sunrise–Moraine Park

"To understand the heart and mind of a person, look not at what he has already achieved, but at what he aspires to."

–Kahlil Gibran

Back Country Skier–
Molas Pass

65

Folsom Field

Junior School Yard Soccer

66

> *"The first question is where are you going?*
> *The second, who is going with you?*
> *The problem lies in reversing the order."*
>
> –A WISEMAN TO HIS FRIEND

Fly Tying–Fly Fishing Camp: Cowdrey, Colorado

The Kinetics Conveyance Race–Boulder Reservoir

The Carriage Driver–Vail

Artist at Varsity Pond

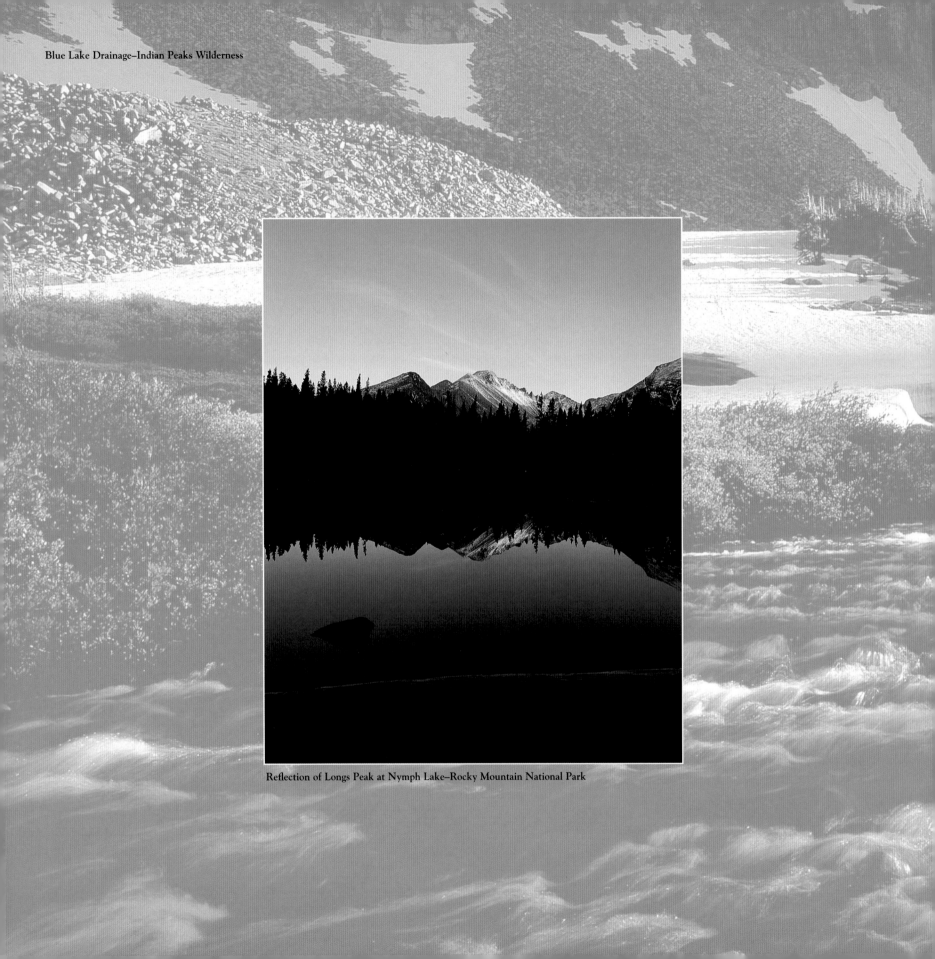

Blue Lake Drainage–Indian Peaks Wilderness

Reflection of Longs Peak at Nymph Lake–Rocky Mountain National Park

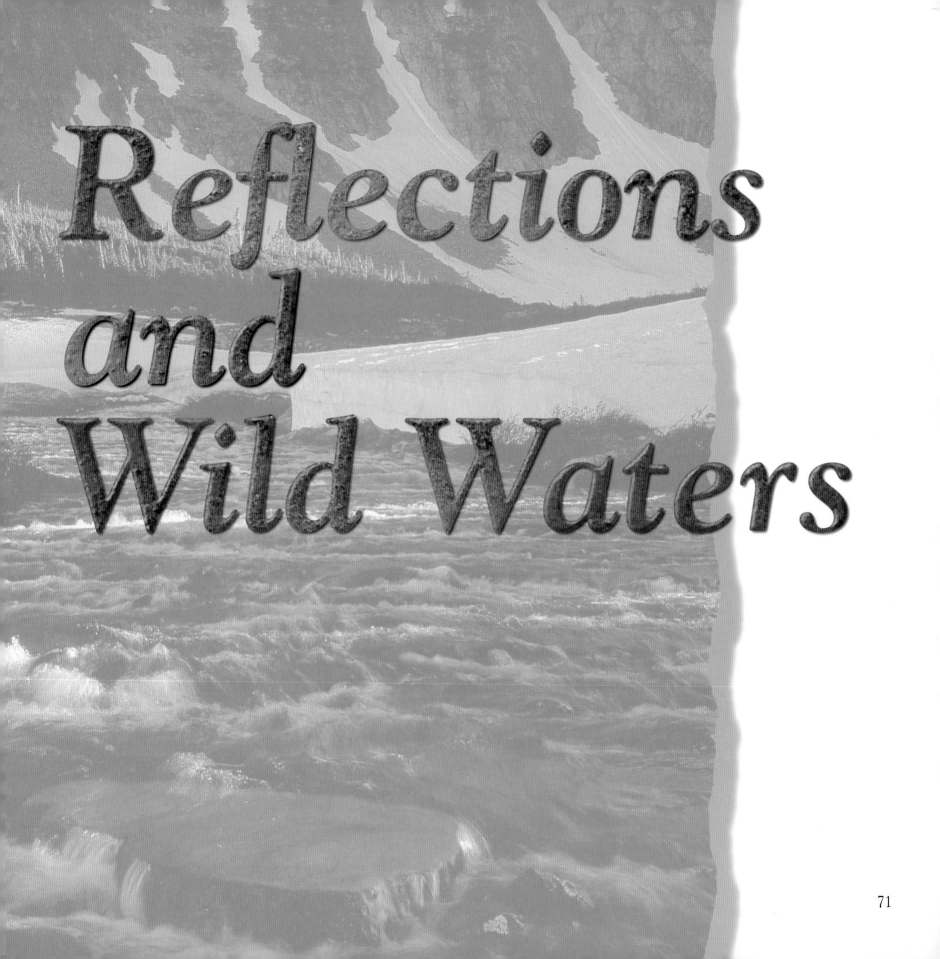

Reflections and Wild Waters

Winter Reflection Maroon Lake–Maroon Bells Wilderness

Reflections

EACH DAY WE LOOK INTO OUR MIRRORS AND SEE A reflection of ourselves we create for others to see. Rare are the days when we walk out of our homes, past the safety of our towns and cities, to seek reflections of ourselves in nature. What might we see that we fear so greatly? To stand at the edge of a pond or lake and to look past the surface where we see only ourselves opens our eyes to a different reflection, a reflection of Colorado's natural beauty so immense that it shatters our domestic notions of beauty.

Reflections born in nature lay in the depths of calm, still waters. They illuminate the grandest of landscapes and the intricate subtleties of detailed patterns. They are often found in fleeting moments that last only as long as the slightest breeze; then they vanish in ripples on the water's surface. Then there are days that linger for hours and allow us to contemplate the depths of our dreams. During the afterglow at dusk, reflections appear in the slow-moving waters of a river; they glare on the frozen suface of a lake in the blasting sunrise, and again in midst of daylight on a rain-filled pool in the desert's slick rock. Reflections tempt us to remain true to Colorado's greater images, until life calls us back from the edge of the wilderness to the comfort of our homes.

Wild Waters

FREE-FLOWING STREAMS AND RIVERS RUSH EAST and west from the heights of the Continental Divide. Born out of winter's snowmelt, or an artesian spring, their clear waters cascade down mountains through meadows into natural lakes and man-made reservoirs. Tributary after tributary join to form larger streams and the great rivers that ultimately reach the seas. Rivers named Arkansas, Animas, Cache La Poudre, Colorado, Dolores, Gunnison, Platte, Rio Grande, Roaring Fork, San Juan and Yampa are legends whose origins are found in Colorado.

These precious waters flow from high in the mountains and spill down through hanging canyons. They flow from the midst of arid climates through some of the driest deserts on the planet out to the Atlantic and Pacific Oceans. Their waters provide for the people of Colorado and for people thousands of miles away in Mexico and the Southeastern United States. Everyday these waters are transported through complex aqueduct systems to irrigate our crops and to produce hydroelectricity for our homes and businesses. These waters are the source of recreation for millions of fishermen, river runners and boaters. The Colorado rivers link our lives to nature. In our own busy worlds, we often overlook their significance. We depend on these rivers for the sustenance that gives rise to our own well-being, and it will take great restraint to sustain and nurture them. The maintenance and well-being of the wild, free-flowing Colorado rivers is our inheritance and our children's legacy.

"As a painter, I become more lucid when confronted by nature."

–CEZANNE

Old Stag in the Yampa River–Deer Lodge Park, Dinosaur National Monument

"You must travel the river, live on it, follow it when there is morning light, and follow it when there is nothing but dark and the banks have blurred into shadows."

—WILL HAYGOOD

Harding Hole I–The Yampa River

"The ever-present phenomenon ceases to exist for our senses. It was a city dweller, or a prisoner, or a blind man suddenly given his sight, who first noted natural beauty."

–GOURMONT

Harding Hole II–The Yampa River

Sunrise Reflection on Ice–Fraser River I

"*The sky is the daily bread of the eyes.*"

—EMERSON

Sunrise Reflection on Ice–Fraser River II

Sunrise on East Boulder Creek–White Cliffs II

Lilies on Big Creek Lake

*"All you need to do to receive guidance
is to ask for it and then listen."*

–SANAYA ROMAN

Lazy Afternoon–Wheeler Lakes, Eagle Nest Wilderness

"As for me, I know of nothing else but miracles."

—WALT WHITMAN

Fall Majesty–Maroon Lake, Maroon Bells Wilderness

Wild Flowers Drainage into Lake Isabelle–Indian Peaks Wilderness

"Water flows from
high in the mountains.
Water runs deep
in the Earth.
Miraculously,
water comes to us,
and sustains all life."
—THICH NHAT HANH

Heart Lake Drainage, Prairie Primrose–East Porthole

Pawnee Peak–Indian Peaks Wilderness II

Lily Pad Crossing–Surprise Lake, Eagles Nest Wilderness

Rippling Brook, Drainage into Lake Isabelle–Indian Peaks Wilderness

"Treat the earth well . . .
it was not given to you by your parents . . .
It was lent to you by your children."
— KENYAN PROVERB

Hayes Creek Falls–The Crystal River

87

Scouting Warm Springs Rapid–The Yampa River

Floating the Yampa River near Tiger Wall

Running the Arkansas above Buena Vista

"I have always known that at last I would take this road,
but yesterday I did not know that it would be today."
—NARIHARA

Running White Water on the The Arkansas River
—Rapid Number I

Fall on the Elk River

"Little minds are interested in the extraordinary; great minds in the commonplace."

–ELBERT HUBBARD

Heavenly Skies–Deer Lodge Park, The Yampa River

"Nature is a mutable cloud, which is always and never the same."

—Ralph Waldo Emerson

"I have amazing news for you.

Man is not alone on this planet. He is part of a community,

upon which he depends absolutely.”

–DANIEL QUINN, ISHMAEL

Hike to Rattlesnake Arches–BLM Land near Fruita
Wilderness Study Area

Anasazi Ruins, Mesa Verde

Parks, Monuments & Wild Places

Colorado Parks, Monuments & Wild Places

WE CAN ONLY IMAGINE WHAT IT MUST HAVE been like to have discovered Colorado 300 years ago. To have found a place so beautiful and diverse must have left explorers awestruck.

One such pioneer, not so long ago, who was responsible in part for the development of the National Park system, made a huge difference in Colorado. Enos Nills founded Rocky Mountain National Park in 1915. His love and enthusiasm for Colorado in the late nineteenth and early twentieth century set the tone for the preservation of the wide open wild places that we know today. Over one third of Colorado is forests or wild lands. Found across Colorado, these parks, momuments, national forests, wildernesses and wild places are managed by federal, state, county and city agencies. They are the stunning backdrop to our cities, towns and resorts. These lands are designated for a range of recreational activities, mineral exploration, tourism, ranching and farming. Everyone who visits or lives in Colorado has a stake in the well-being of these lands. These places are the bedrock values that open the gateway to the vast western landscape and make Colorado one of the greatest places on earth.

These places are more than short stops for visitors on vacation; they are the wilderness of America's landscape today as we have defined it in the National Parks Act of 1872 and the Wilderness Act of 1964. Not only do they provide places for us to recreate and vacation, they are also fragile ecosystems where many undomesticated plants and wildlife live. Without these wild places, the water that sustains us would not rush forth to support our towns and cities, and we can not separate our connection from them. Beyond our physical needs these places provide for us they refresh our spirits and remind us of our place in the natural world. They connect us to our history, back to the time when they were inhabited by native cultures. They are windows through which we view the earth's geologic heritage. They are a wellspring for our awe, reverence and understanding of the greater forces of nature at work.

The Proposed Colorado Wilderness Act of 1999

GIVEN CONGRESSIONAL APPROVAL OF THE PROPOSED Colorado Wilderness Act of 1999, more than 1.4 million acres of BLM (Bureau of Land Management) and National Forest land in prime desert canyon country will be protected forever. This represents fifteen percent of 8.4 million acres of public lands managed by the BLM. Skyrocketing population and the increasing popularity of backcountry recreation place intense pressures on the existing wilderness. Protecting these lands will provide critical habitat for 170 rare species and plant communities such as the Kit Fox. Many of these species and habitats cannot be found anyplace else in the world. The natural cultural and scientific resources, such as the ancient Anasazi ruins of Colorado's Cross Canyon, the Vermillion Basin Pertoglyph panels, and the fossil beds in South Shale Ridge, will be protected from vandalism. Preserved areas provide Coloradans access to backcountry recreation, promote tourism, and attract businesses to the high quality of life available in our communities. The preservation of these pristine landscapes and spectacular vistas benefit our children and future generations to come. This is the citizens' wilderness proposal for undiscovered lands of the BLM. This proposal needs the support of everyone who can reach out to give a hand to ensure its approval.

"A wilderness, in contrast with those areas where man and his own works dominate the landscape, is hereby recognized as an area where the earth and its community of life are untrampled by man, where man himself is a visitor who does not remain."

–1964 WILDERNESS ACT

Wagon Wheel Point–The Yampa

Overlook at Big Joe Rapid–The Yampa River, Dinosaur National Monument

"*Me imperturbe, standing at ease in Nature.*"
—WALT WHITMAN

Black Rocks in Horse Thief Canyon–Colorado River

Snow Squall over Great Sand Dunes National Monument

Broken Hill–Big Blue Wilderne

"Grant me the ability to be alone. May it be my custom to go outdoors each day among the trees and grasses, among all growing things and there may I be alone, and enter into prayer to talk with the one that I belong to."

–RABBI NACHMAN OF BRATZLAV

Daybreak at Deer Lodge Park–The Yampa

Last Light on the Dunes–Great Sand Dunes
National Monument

Sunset over the Sangre de Cristos–Great Sand Dunes
National Monument

"All colors are the friends of their neighbors and the lovers of their opposites."

–CHAZAL

Medano Creek–Great Sand Dunes
National Monument

103

Great Horned Owl on Farm House–San Luis Valley

"One can never consent to creep when one feels an impulse to soar."

–Helen Keller

Walking against the Grain–Whooping and Sandhill Cranes, Monte Vista Wildlife Refuge I

"The afternoon knows what the morning never suspected."
—SWEDISH PROVERB

Sunrise at Garden of the Gods—Colorado Springs

Shrouded Red Rocks–Garden of the Gods, Colorado Springs

Winter Sunrise–Roxborough State Park

Migrating Elk–Moraine Park, Rocky Mountain National Park

"*If you know wilderness
in the way that you know love,
you would be unwilling to let it go.
We are talking about the body of the beloved,
not real estate.*"

–TERRY TEMPEST WILLIAMS

Winter Refuge–Moraine Park, Rocky Mountain National Park

The Maiden–Boulder Mountain Parks

"If you foolishly ignore beauty you'll soon find yourself without it . . . but if you wisely invest in beauty, it will remain with you all the days of your life."

—Frank Lloyd Wright

Keyhole Arch–Rattlesnake Canyon

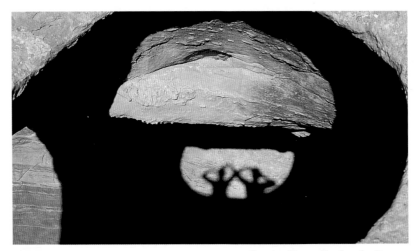

Dancing Figures–Rattlesnake Canyon

"The finest workers in stone are not copper or steel tools, but the gentle touches of air and water working at their leisure with a liberal allowance of time."

–HENRY DAVID THOREAU

*"The most beautiful thing
we can experience
is the mysterious."*
–ALBERT EINSTEIN

Moonset over Red Rock Lake–Indian Peaks Wilderness

Crystal River Mill Site–Raggeds Wilderness

Encroaching Fog & Lights–Mesa Verde

"Give me the splendid silent sun
with all his beams full dazzling!"
—WALT WHITMAN

Mount Yale from Cottonwood Creek–Collegiate Peaks Wilderness

"A hundred years ago, even fifty years ago, it did not seem urgent that we understand the relationship between business and a healthy environment, because natural resources seemed unlimited."

—Paul Hawken

Durango Silverton–Narrow Gauge Train

The Commerce In Ecology

Amtrack along the Colorado in Ruby–Horse Thief Canyon

The Commerce in Ecology

AS WE ENTER THE TWENTY-FIRST CENTURY, Colorado is fortunate to have as robust an economy as it has ever known, and, if the indicators are accurate, one of the strongest in the country. Growth has reached an all-time high at a torrid rate, and unemployment is the lowest in the state's history. Businesses are moving here for many reasons, one of these being the quality of life and natural beauty Colorado offers. Fortunately, early stewards had the foresight to preserve vast sections of land to protect Colorado's natural attributes. These ecologically-oriented values play into Colorado's most recent successes. Yet, the pressures of success are beginning to have a significant impact on our exquisite natural surroundings. Some pragmatists attribute this impact directly to population growth. Colorado's population will have almost doubled from 2.2 million in 1970 to 4.2 million in the year 2000. In forty years an estimated 8.5 million people will live here. How do we balance population growth, economic development and prosperity while preserving the environment? Many complex factors must be weighed, including our quality of life and our economic well-being.

Sustainable Development, A Viable Solution

Sustainable development is a viable solution that has moved to the forefront for many educators, politicians and urban planners. We are fortunate in this day and age to enjoy sophisticated import/export systems that bring food, water and electricity to our homes and businesses. We can exist in some of the most unihabit-

120

able, arid climates and live comfortably. Without these systems, life could not be sustained at the same level simply because the local resource base of the natural environment could not support us, especially in Colorado. The local and global well-being of the natural environment is directly tied to our own. Paul Hawkins, author of *The Ecology of Commerce*, defines sustainability as an "economic state where the demands placed on the environment by people and commerce can be met without reducing the capacity of the environment to provide for future generations." Developing environmentally responsibile values, ethics, principles and practices in our homes, businesses and communities makes a difference for a healthy Colorado. Both organizations and private citizens are coming forward in an effort to spread the word and effect change

in Colorado. Colorado Business for Social Responsiblity supports responsible business practices, ethics and values to maintain a healthy environment. Eco-Cycle of Boulder focuses its educational and operational efforts by decreasing solid waste disposal through increased recycling on a grass-roots level. The Earthlaw Environmental Law Clinic at the University of Denver "fights to save animals and ecosystems that cannot defend themselves." The Colorado Sustainablity Project's vision for a "Sustainable Colorado" promotes "planning today for a shared tomorrow: creating principles and partnerships for Colorado's future." These are only a few of the organizations devoted to a planned approach to sustain the health of Colorado today and for future generations in the next millenium.

Whitehead Peak through Molas MineTressel

High Country Range Land beneath the Gore Range

Fence Line and Old Barn
–Durango

Colorado State Capitol

Denver Skyline at Sunrise II

Roof Line at Denver International Airport

"Better values build better equity."

–Thomas M. Chappell

Moonrise on the Denver Skyline from Speer Boulevard–Denver

Denver Skyline from City Park Lake

Retired Old Chevy

Old Barn and Farm House on the Front Range

"Earth and sky, woods and fields, lakes and rivers,
the mountains and the seas, are excellent schoolmasters, and
teach some of us more than we can ever learn from books."

—JOHN LUBBOCK

Spiral Staircase at Old Main–

The Quad at Old Main–

Sunrise at LASP-CU Research Center, Boulder

Macky Auditorium from the Quad–
University of Colorado, Boulder

High Holiday Lights–
Chautauqua Park, Boulder

View from the North Peak toward Breckenridge at Keystone Ski Area

Holiday Trimmings at Friendly Fire–Fort Collins

130

Ski School at Keystone

"…even in the day of vast
cities and powerful machines,
the good earth is our mother,
and if we destroy her
we destroy ourselves."
—PAUL B. SEARS

Saint Regis Hotel and Ajax at Aspen

Fireworks Closing Ceremonies–
The World Ski Championship 1999, Vail

Denver City and
County Building–Denver

133

"There is nothing more real in this life than land. Earth gives us each thing we have, and at the end we return those gifts to it. 'Owning land' is a relatively modern notion and by no means a universal practice. In fact, to many of the world's peoples who live intimately with the land, the idea of ownership is incomprehensible. The search for good land is like the search for a mate. We certainly hope to find sustenance, partnership, comfort and stability. In the end, if we truly wish to settle peacefully and productively, we must find love and passion for the land as well."

–Michael Potts

Mineral Hot Springs–San Luis Valley

Great Horned Owl In Flight

The Afterwords

Matters of Deep Concern

Colorado faces many challenges as the year 2000 comes to pass. Colorado's economy is at an all-time high and the population is rising faster than ever as it becomes known how wonderful it is to live in this place. Land is being developed throughout the state at an unparalleled rate. Non-renewable energy sources and supplies are being depleted. Traffic is a major concern in our cities and towns at every turn. Pressure on our most precious natural treasures — in our forests, parks, rivers, mountains, deserts and prairie grasslands — continue to mount. This is a semi-arid climate that supplies water for 4.2 million people and millions more downstream. The air we breathe and see is becoming more polluted. Acid rain is becoming a problem for habitat in the higher climbs of our state. Crime is at an all-time high and violent crime has become an everyday occurrence. With more than 8 million people to inhabit the state by the year 2040 (twice as many as today) these issues may pale in comparison to those that lay ahead. The problems appear daunting and new imaginative leadership and solutions are needed. The solutions are as varied as those who propose them. It may take a few dedicated and conscious people to create a movement to sustain a quality of life that does not erode as we continue to share this wonderful place with an increasing amount of people. It will take more people meeting to discuss their concerns, creating individual commitments and forming new partnerships to make change. Change is the only way for us to find new ways to break through the bottlenecks. Each of us will be forced to participate regardless of our beliefs and baseline perspectives. Ultimately, it will be our responsibility to face these challenges together, make a difference and become involved any way possible. It only takes one step through the door to find out that what we have feared for so long is easy to learn anew. We must remember the earth, our beloved planet, sustains us all. We, in turn, must nurture her soul for own well-being and for the generations who will inherit our legacy.

About the Photographs

I make photographs of Colorado and her people because I love this place. I drove into Colorado in my 1967 VW bug in October of 1993 on I-70 for the first time when I was 19 years old and my love affair with Colorado began immediately. As it was then and remains to this day, I viewed the landscape as I passed it with great awe. It wasn't until I moved to Leadville in February 1974 that I began to understand the scope and breadth of Colorado's magnificence. I started making photographs of Colorado in 1985. I have chased to as many places across the state as possible to capture the essence of its grandeur and the depths of its most intimate natural wonders. I often drive the most remote roads, scenic byways, raft wild and scenic rivers and backpack or hike into places to make photographs. I often visit a location a number of times waiting for just the right atmospheric conditions and lighting to capture an image. Most of the images are made at the edge of dawn or dusk, or in the midst of a storm or just after it has cleared. Sometimes without warning I stumble into a scene without planning and experience a situation that yields rarest finds. I have learned that taking risks in pushing the limits of photographic technique has created the most unusual effects and spectacular photos. These moments are the most precious times when fate and creation collide. Inspiration appears magically, making for the happiest photographs and the fine art of photography a fulfilling pleasure.

I use Nikon 35mm cameras and lenses along with a Pentax 6 x 7 medium format camera and lenses. The film chosen most often is Fuji Velvia. Composition, exposure and film speed all vary depending upon the setting, subject and light. I use a simple technique of researching a subject or location, setting up, composing, exposing, then waiting. With a little luck, much anticipation and persistence, the greater powers of life bring forth the beauty every time.

Special Thanks

This past year my father passed away. I owe him a debt of gratitude for making life possible and special heart felt thanks for always being there. Dads are simply there for those of us who know them no matter how trying the times. I miss you Dad.

To all those friends, acquaintances and professionals, I offer my most gracious and humble "thank you" for your support, help and encouragement. These people include: Deborah Moran, Dave Dombrowski, Betty Taylor, Len Krueger, Susan Zvarda, Tony Lazarine, Crista Newmeyer, Geri Lynn Baumblatt, Lori Swingle of the Denver Public Library, Jay Kennis, Zale Gaylen, Colorado Congressman — Mark Udall, David Solzman, Ray Castellino, and Julianne Parrett. For all those who have given of themselves in one way or another to support my efforts during this time and I have not listed your name, "Thank You."